THE FLYING
AND OTHER STR

The *Oxford Progressive English Readers* series provides a wide range of reading for learners of English.

Each book in the series has been written to follow the strict guidelines of a syllabus, wordlist and structure list. The texts are graded according to these guidelines; Grade 1 at a 1,400 word level, Grade 2 at a 2,100 word level, Grade 3 at a 3,100 word level, Grade 4 at a 3,700 word level and Grade 5 at a 5,000 word level.

The latest methods of text analysis, using specially designed software, ensure that readability is carefully controlled at every level. Any new words which are vital to the mood and style of the story are explained within the text, and reoccur throughout for maximum reinforcement. New language items are also clarified by attractive illustrations.

Each book has a short section containing carefully graded exercises and controlled activities, which test both global and specific understanding.

The Flying Heads and Other Strange Stories

Edited by David Foulds

Hong Kong
Oxford University Press
Oxford Singapore Tokyo

Oxford University Press

Oxford New York Toronto
Kuala Lumpur Singapore Hong Kong Tokyo
Delhi Bombay Calcutta Madras Karachi
Nairobi Dar es Salaam Cape Town
Melbourne Auckland Madrid

and associated companies in
Berlin Ibadan

Oxford is a trade mark of Oxford University Press

First published 1993
Second impression 1994

© Oxford University Press 1993

All rights reserved. No part of this publication may be reproduced,
stored in a retrieval system, or transmitted, in any form or by any means,
without the prior permission in writing of Oxford University Press
(Hong Kong) Ltd. Within Hong Kong, exceptions are allowed in respect
of any fair dealing for the purpose of research or private study,
or criticism or review, as permitted under the Copyright Ordinance
currently in force. Enquiries concerning reproduction outside
these terms and in other countries should be sent to
Oxford University Press (Hong Kong) Ltd at the address below

This book is sold subject to the condition that it shall not, by way of
trade or otherwise, be lent, re-sold, hired out or otherwise circulated
without the publisher's prior consent in any form of binding or cover
other than that in which it is published and without a similar condition
including this condition being imposed on the subsequent purchaser

Illustrated by Wu Siu Kau

Syllabus designer: David Foulds

Text processing and analysis by Luxfield Consultants Ltd.

ISBN 0 19 585495 0

Printed in Hong Kong
Published by Oxford University Press (Hong Kong) Ltd
18/F Warwick House, Taikoo Place, 979 King's Road,
Quarry Bay, Hong Kong

CONTENTS

1	THE FLYING HEADS	1
2	A SAILOR'S STORY	10
3	UNHAPPY MRS LEE	20
4	THE BAKER'S WIFE	30
5	AFTER MIDNIGHT	38
6	THE MYSTERIOUS ILLNESS	47
7	THE LEOPARD MAN	55
8	THE WISE MAN OF NAGASAKI	63
	QUESTIONS AND ACTIVITIES	70

1

THE FLYING HEADS

Walking through lonely places

A young man was walking along a path beside a stream. He had a walking-stick in his hand, and he was carrying an old bag. He wore a large hat on his head, and a pair of old sandals on his feet. He was going home. His journey was a long one, but he was not in a hurry to finish it.

He had a good reason for not wanting to hurry. He had failed the government examinations and he knew he had to explain this to his parents. This was something that he did not like doing! He had studied in the capital city for three years, and he had failed the examinations twice. So he did not choose the shortest road home, and he did not choose the easiest way. Instead, he walked through lonely places; places which he had only heard about and had never visited before.

The young man's name was Hoa Phieu.

The path followed the stream into the mountains. It twisted so often that soon Hoa Phieu was completely lost. He had no idea where he was. However, he was sure that he would meet someone and then he could ask for help.

Although the path twisted so often, he knew he was travelling south; and that was the direction of home. Hoa kept walking along the path. Suddenly it turned and went away from the stream. It led straight up a hill, through a lot of trees and bushes. The only sounds he could hear were those of birds and insects.

Somewhere to sleep

In the hot sun, Hoa climbed up the steep path. Soon he was very tired. He began to think about where he would sleep that night. He could not see anywhere for a person to live in that lonely place, but he still hoped that the path would lead him to a house. And so he went on cheerfully.

At the top of the hill there were not so many trees and bushes. Hoa saw a tall stone building above him. It stood on the top of the hill, high above the next valley. When he was close to it, Hoa saw that it was very old. Parts of the building had begun to fall down. Its white stones shone in the light of the evening sun. Plants grew on the old walls and moved gently in the evening wind.

Hoa climbed through a hole in one of the broken walls. He saw a wide, open space. It was a courtyard. There was a stone well in the centre, and small buildings around the sides. Hoa looked at one of the small buildings. It did not look as lonely as the rest of the place. It had strong walls and a proper roof. Perhaps someone lived there. Hoa was happy. He had found somewhere to sleep that night.

The old man

He went to the door of the small building and looked inside. After a moment, his eyes became used to the darkness. He could see a shape on the other side of the room. Someone was sitting there. Hoa took off his hat; next he put down his bag and leaned his walking-stick against the wall outside. Then he made a polite bow and stepped into the room. An old man was sitting on a mat in the corner. There was no hair on his head,

but he had a long, thin, grey beard.
He wore a long, old coat which was brown now but once, long ago, was probably yellow.

Hoa greeted him, but the old man said nothing. He only smiled. Without speaking, the old man pointed to a second mat. It was lying against the wall by the door. Hoa sat down. Still the old man did not speak. Hoa stayed silent too, and rested. Soon it began to get dark. Hoa did not feel so tired, so he stood up.

'Don't be afraid'

'Where are you going?' asked the old man suddenly.
 'To wash in that well,' replied Hoa with surprise.
 'Do not do that,' said the old man at once. 'You must wash only in the flowing water of the stream. But you can't go there now; it is getting too dark.'

After a while the old man said, 'Bring your walking-stick inside.'

Hoa was very surprised. He thought about the old man's words, but did not know what they meant. But he obeyed the old man, and brought the stick inside. Then night came. The sun went down, darkness fell and a gentle wind began to blow.

The old man lit a lamp and gave Hoa some food — a small amount of cold rice and some weak tea. Then he lay down to sleep with his face to the wall. After a while, he turned his head and said to Hoa, 'If anything happens in the night, don't be afraid. Just do nothing, and you will be quite safe. I do not think anything will happen, but I want to tell you this so that you will be safe. You must not go outside for any reason. Don't even go near the window or the door.'

The old man turned his head towards the wall again and went to sleep.

Hoa did not go to sleep at once. He looked through the large, empty window into the darkness. There was nothing there. Nothing strange was going to happen in that quiet place, he told himself. Soon his eyes began to close and he fell asleep.

Screams in the night

Suddenly there were terrible screams coming from the valley below; they woke Hoa. There was fear in the screams, and fierce anger as well. They were so loud that Hoa stopped breathing for a moment. Then, in the light of the moon, he saw things flying through the air. Suddenly he realized that they were human heads. Their long, black hair moved in the wind. The screams were coming from their wide-open mouths.

The heads flew by, one by one. In the distance, Hoa could see a dark cloud of heads hanging over the valley. There were hundreds of them.

One head flew close to the window. It stopped suddenly and stared inside. Its face was very pale. Its large, still eyes were red. Its long, black hair was blowing in the wind. In its open mouth, Hoa saw sharp teeth. For a long moment, the face stared at the frightened young man. Then it shook itself angrily and flew away.

The proud people

The old man had woken while this was happening. He waited until Hoa was not so frightened. Then he poured him a cup of tea and said, 'I did not tell you about the heads because I hoped they would not come tonight. That is why I said nothing to you. But now you have seen them, so I will tell you everything.'

The old man was silent. He looked out at the night for a long time, and then continued.

'A long time ago,' he said, 'some people lived in our mountains. They came here from another country. They were clever people and they lived in peace. They worked hard and lived in comfort. But these people were also proud and brave. They wanted to live by themselves, and they refused to obey the rule of the king. For many years they fought with great bravery against the king's soldiers. However, they lost a lot of their land. They had no time to work in their fields, and the long war made them unhappy. So, in the end, they stopped fighting and tried to make peace with the king. But the king was angry. Because of the long war, many of his best men were dead. Also, he was afraid that he would soon have to fight these proud people again. So the king ordered his soldiers to kill every one of them — old men, women and children. Hundreds died. Very few of them escaped.'

The ghosts

The old man looked sadly out into the darkness again and then continued his story:

'The flying heads which you saw belong to the ghosts of the people he killed. In the day-time, these ghosts look like people, but at night their heads leave their bodies and fly above the valley. They hunt for living people so that they can punish them for their cruel deaths long ago. They cannot enter any place where people live. They can only kill people who are outside their houses at night. But they can also destroy anyone who leaves something outside his house. This may be something that belongs to him, or something that he has touched. When the heads find something like that outside a house, they take it and use it to kill the careless owner.'

The old man finished speaking and sat still. Hoa also sat still. He was thinking about the cruel and terrible story. He was glad he had obeyed the old man, and brought his walking stick into the house.

Hoa in danger

Suddenly he heard a terrible scream, much louder than before. Another head appeared at the window, its hair blowing behind it in the wind. Hoa was frightened, and dropped his cup. A little stream of tea began to flow across the stone floor. The head noticed it. At once it shook itself and flew to the door.

It watched eagerly as the stream of tea came towards it. Hoa also noticed what was happening. It was his tea, and it was going outside, towards the terrible head. He was so frightened that he could not move. He could not look away from the stream of tea moving slowly towards the door.

Then suddenly, with surprising speed, the old man jumped up. With a corner of his long old coat, he stopped the spilt tea just before it ran under the door. When the head saw what the old man was doing, it turned angrily and flew away.

The rest of the night was peaceful.

Dead or alive?

In the morning, the old man woke Hoa and said, 'I will go with you down into the valley. I can show you the way out of this part of the country. You will not find anywhere else here to stay for another night, and you have already seen how dangerous it is.'

A path led along the side of the mountain and down into the valley. As soon as they stepped out from the trees and bushes, they saw a village in front of them. At first Hoa was glad to see it. Then he realized that there was something wrong with the village. The houses had no walls or roofs. The people who lived there were strange as well. Although they looked strong and healthy, they were not doing anything. They stood around or sat by their houses. They did not speak and they did not notice Hoa and the old man. They just stared in front of them, not looking at anything. Were they dead or alive?

'These are the people I told you about,' said the old man. 'I know them because they have red eyes. There are several villages full of people like this.

These people are not dead, and they are not alive either. A few old people like myself live among them.'

Escape from the valley of the ghosts

Hoa felt sad at what he saw. He said, 'Can't anyone free them from this terrible life?'

The old man slowly shook his head and said, 'Perhaps only time can free them. Time changes everything. In the end people forget even the most cruel things. One day these poor people, too, will forget the terrible things that happened to them.'

Then he led the young man far away from the village, to a river. He showed Hoa a place to cross, and said goodbye.

'Cross to the other side of the river, and you will be safe. Go home to your mother and father, young man, and live in happiness and peace.'

A Sailor's Story

The trader

Many years ago, when I was still a young man, I sailed on a ship going to China. I was looking for trade. All I wanted at that time was to be rich and famous. At first the wind was blowing in the right direction, and we sailed along at a good speed. I was thinking happily of the money I was going to make. Then the weather changed. Terrible clouds filled the sky, and a fierce wind blew from the west. There was nothing we could do. The wind blew us far away from where we were going.

For ten days we sailed on, blown by the wind through an unknown sea. Then at last we saw land. No one knew where we were, or the name of the land we saw. But we needed food and water very badly. We stopped at a place where a river flowed into the sea. We took a small boat and rowed to the shore. We hoped that the people of the land were friendly.

Greed

We were met by a crowd of people with smiling faces. They happily gave us food and water. Even better, I saw that they had houses full of goods that they had not made themselves — many more than they could ever use. I was sure that they had traded with someone. I decided to go up the river to try to find the traders myself.

I chose eight sailors to row the boat, and I took lots of different goods to trade. Very early the next morning, we tried to set off on our journey. But as we climbed into our boat, the villagers came to talk to us. They said it was too dangerous to go up the river. They even gave us presents to stop us going.

I thought I knew why they did this. They were afraid that if we traded with the people up the river, prices would get higher. How wrong I was! How greedy and stupid!

The rich village

We did not listen to the villagers. We got into our boats and left.

The journey was very long. Trees had fallen into the river, making it very hard to travel. At the time, all I could think about was reaching the next village. Then I could trade. If I had been less stupid, I would have seen that the trees had not fallen down by themselves. Someone had cut them down. Someone wanted to stop people going up the river. Or to stop something coming down it.

At last, just before night came, we saw a village at the side of the river. It looked richer than the other village. The houses were made of wood, and stood on long posts in the water at the side of the river. A cool wind blew through the trees. I thought I would enjoy spending the night there.

A kind welcome

When we arrived at the village, the people came running to meet us. They looked at us with interest, and began talking loudly to each other. Of course none

of us could understand what they were saying. I made
another big mistake. I thought they were happy because
we had brought them good things to trade. If only I
had thought about it carefully! But all I cared about was
money. They made movements with their hands that
seemed to welcome us. And they seemed to be making
some food for us. We were all very pleased.

After a delicious feast, the villagers took us to their
houses. They led each man into a separate house. This
did not seem quite right to me, but I did not stop it. I
did not want their kindness to end. Anyway, the houses
were not far from each other. The men in each house
could hear what was happening in all the other houses.
And we all had guns. I was quite sure we would not
be beaten if there was a fight. I went into the biggest
house. I was not afraid.

A strange silence

The house was standing in the river like the others. To
go inside you did not climb a ladder or some stairs.
Instead, there was a plank — a wide, flat piece of wood
— that you walked up as if you
were walking up a hill.

For the first time, I began to ask myself some questions about these people. Any kind of animal could climb up a piece of wood like this. Weren't these people afraid of snakes, or crocodiles? Either they were very stupid, or they were very fierce. Perhaps even the river animals were afraid of them. Still, it was too late to go back now. I held my gun tightly in my hand. I decided to stay awake that night. I did not want to be killed in my sleep.

But the villagers must have put something in my food at the feast. As soon as I lay down, I began to feel very sleepy. I tried and tried to stay awake, but it was no good. I just had time to put my gun safely by the side of my bed. Then everything went black.

I do not know how long I slept. I do not even know why I woke up, but it saved my life. At once I noticed the strange silence. There was no sound at all. By the light of the moon, I could see that there was no one in the room. Where had the people gone? Then I heard a noise. It was coming from under the floor of the house. I crept from my bed and looked down through a small hole where the pieces of wood in the floor came together. I saw what was making the noise. I stopped breathing.

Crocodiles

Below me, hardly two metres away, were many crocodiles. The great, ugly animals were sliding and crawling over each other's wet bodies. I trembled from head to foot. Even if you have a gun, a crocodile is a frightening enemy. They are so big and so heavy, and they can move very fast. In the water, they are silent and strong. If they catch you near water, you will probably die. They are the most terrifying animals in the world. And the only way out of the house was to walk along that plank, over the river. I would only live if I ran very fast, and shot at the crocodiles with my gun.

I reached for my gun. It wasn't there. I could not find it anywhere in the house. I wanted to cry. I thought, 'The family in this house must have taken my gun so that they could run away themselves.'

Nowhere to run to

Then I thought some more. Why was there no sound — not even any screams or cries of people being eaten? Had the crocodiles eaten all the villagers already? Perhaps I had been woken up by a scream. Or perhaps they were too afraid of these terrible animals to make a sound.

What about my friends? They would certainly have shouted to each other that there were crocodiles. Were they all dead too?

I began to shout, hoping to hear someone answer me. I felt so alone. And how I hated the noise of those horrible, crawling wet bodies below me!

But it was a stupid thing to do. When I shouted, the crocodiles began to crawl towards the door of the house. More and more came crawling from all directions. There were hundreds of them. Now the strongest crocodiles were already climbing up the plank. They were coming towards me across the floor!

I wanted to run, but there was nowhere to go. I looked round for something to help me. I could feel their hot breath on my legs. In a moment their strong teeth would bite me. I was going to die.

A hard fight

My fear made me strong. I pulled a long stick from the roof of the house. As the first crocodile opened its terrible mouth, I pushed the stick down its throat. Warm blood flowed out of its mouth. It twisted back in pain, and moved away from me.

The next crocodile attacked. This one must have been very old. It was the biggest I had ever seen. Its small, black eyes were full of hate. I looked at it — and I felt as if I had seen those eyes before.

Before I had time to think, I felt a terrible pain. I looked down, and saw that the crocodile had my leg in its teeth. I screamed. I hardly knew what I was doing. The pain was so bad, I could hardly see.

I used my stick to hit the animal on its teeth, again and again. Somehow I hit it hard enough to hurt it.

It opened its mouth to cry out, and I quickly pulled my leg away. I was free.

I pushed hard against the wall of the
house, and it broke. In terrible pain, I
somehow climbed down a post and
jumped across the water onto the ground. Then, with
my stick to help me, I was able to walk to a tree.

Using my hands and my one good leg, I climbed to
the top of the tree. I tied myself to it with my belt. I
hung in the tree like that for hours. I was too weak to
move and too frightened to sleep.

Nothing has changed

At last, morning came. Girls climbed down from the houses to fetch water. As they passed the tree, they saw me. Some of them pointed at me in surprise. Some of them shouted and ran back to the village.

Soon, some young men hurried towards me. They carried me to the village. I was taken to the same house that I had left the night before. To my surprise, everything looked the same as when I had first arrived. Even the wall, which I had broken through to get away, had been mended.

Everybody in the house ran towards me. They leaned over me and spoke to each other in their own language. But I could not speak to them. When I asked them why they had taken my gun, and where my friends were, they did not understand me. Although they seemed very kind, I felt more and more uneasy. I did not want to stay there until I was well again.

The village chief

Suddenly the village chief walked into the house. He was a very old man, taller and fatter than any of the others. But when I had seen him at the feast, the night before, his face had seemed different. Now it was round and red and looked very painful. When he spoke to tell the others to go away, I saw that almost all of his teeth were broken.

I began to think that I knew what had happened. But it was so horrible, so terrifying, that I would not believe it. Then the chief made me understand that he wanted to look at my bad leg. His face moved closer and closer to it. He was smelling it. At the same time he opened his small, black eyes and looked at me.

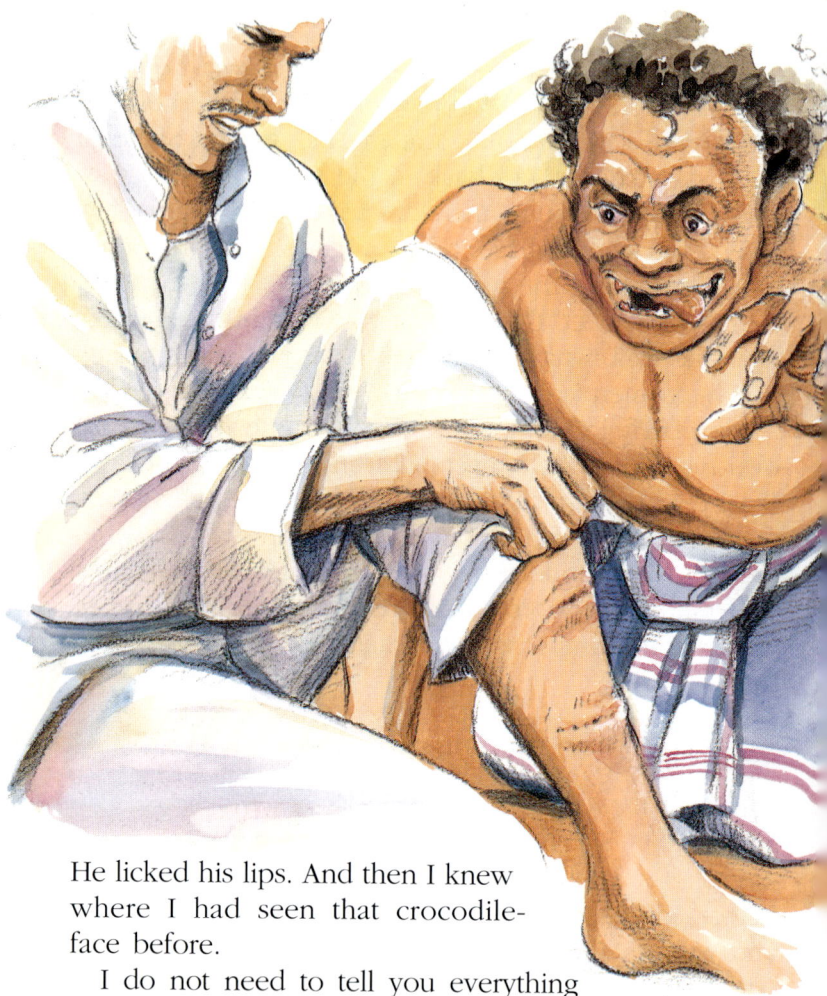

He licked his lips. And then I knew where I had seen that crocodile-face before.

I do not need to tell you everything
5 that happened that day. But you will not be surprised to read that as soon as I could, I crept out of the house. I went as fast as I could towards my boat.

On my way, I saw a crowd of women, crying over a dead man's body. He was lying on the ground. It
10 looked as if his throat had been hurt. I was sure that I knew how he had died.

The terrible truth

When at last I arrived at my boat, I got in quickly and began to row. I did not wait for my friends. I knew that they were as dead as they could be. It must have been one of their screams that had woken me. I could not think about them, and the horrible way they had died.

It was a long journey before I arrived at the first village. I was weak and tired, and my hands would not stop trembling. Rowing was very hard for me. When I landed, for a moment I was afraid of the smiling people. Who knew what secrets they had? Then I found someone who could speak a few words of English. His face grew white with fear at the word 'crocodile'. He looked up the river and trembled when I said it.

He looked after my leg very well. After a week I was strong enough to travel. The man took me to my ship and I told the sailors to set off at once. We sailed safely to China, and back again.

That is the end of my story. I shall never forget it. The people I tell it to never forget it either. Remember, there are people in this world who are crocodiles. During the day they look like people. But if they are kind to you, it is because they love the smell of your blood. That is the truth. Just look at my leg, and you will see.

3

UNHAPPY MRS LEE

A happy life

Kuo Yu lived in a town in Shantung. It was his home and he was happy there. He did many different jobs, but he went most often to the market. He found plenty of work there. Sometimes he took messages from one person to another, sometimes he helped to carry goods into the shops. He always earned enough money to buy rice and tea. Sometimes he even had enough money to buy beer, which he liked very much.

One day he sat drinking beer with his friends. They were telling each other stories — some of them very frightening and strange. But nothing frightened Kuo. He laughed at his friends, and argued that such things could not really happen. They talked for hours. The friends did not say goodbye and go home until it was very late at night.

The strange lady

Kuo walked back towards his house, alone. He was a little drunk. He had had too much beer to drink. The moon shone above the quiet, narrow streets of the town. Some places were well lit, but in others there were dark shadows.

Kuo walked along a lane towards a temple which was near where he lived. Suddenly he saw something strange. Someone came out of the temple and started walking down the centre of the lane towards him. But it was very late. Kuo knew that the temple was closed at that time.

Kuo stopped and thought to himself, 'Who is this walking around so late at night?' He stepped back into the dark shadows and waited.

The person came closer, and Kuo could see that it was a woman. The bright moonlight shone on her as she came nearer. Her clothes were those of a rich lady. She was tall and thin and she wore a long, loose dress and a blue jacket. She moved very lightly and made no sound. It seemed as if she wasn't walking at all, but flying just above the ground. The wind was blowing her along. But then Kuo saw that the leaves in the trees were still. There was no wind.

The light in the window

The woman did not look at Kuo as she went past him.
Her dark eyes stared from her pale face.
Her face was as white as a ghost!

'That lady looks as if she's mad,' thought Kuo to himself. 'Why is she walking about at night without a servant? How mysterious. I'll follow her, and see where she goes.'

The strange woman was moving quickly. Kuo had to run to follow her. She moved faster and faster, and then suddenly disappeared into a narrow lane. Kuo ran as quickly as he could. When he looked into the narrow lane, there was no one there. He was just in time to hear a door close — but which one? Kuo did not know. There were no gates open, and he could not hear anyone moving around. He crept carefully along the lane from gate to gate. He was looking for somewhere to get in.

At last, at the end of the lane, he found a very old gate. It was not open, but it was broken. Kuo could easily squeeze through. On the other side was a small courtyard. A light shone in a window. Kuo crept quietly across the courtyard to the window and looked into the room.

Unhappy Mrs Lee

A woman was sitting at a small table. There was a teapot and some cups on the table, and an oil lamp. She sighed sadly.

'Well, that's not her,' said Kuo to himself. 'That's Mrs Lee. Poor lady, she must be very unhappy.' He knew that Mrs Lee's husband had gone away on a long journey. He left just after they were married, and he never came back. She was always very sad. She did not know why her husband had never returned.

Kuo felt ashamed, looking into someone else's room. He decided to go. But just then he saw the strange lady inside the room. She was standing there, silent and still.

'How can those two women know each other?' Kuo asked himself.

He stood quietly at the window and watched with interest. At first nothing happened. The strange lady just stood in the corner of the room. Mrs Lee stared into the empty air above the oil lamp and sighed sadly.

A rope

After some time, the strange lady stepped forward without a sound. Her dark eyes stared at Mrs Lee. Her white face was still; Kuo did not know if she was sad or happy, angry or frightened. Slowly the strange lady pulled a rope from the loose sleeve of her dress. Then she tied it into a noose. She still stared at Mrs Lee and slowly moved closer to her. At the same time she lifted the rope high into the air in front of her.

Kuo almost stopped breathing. He no longer felt at all drunk.

'Is that woman going to kill poor Mrs Lee?' he asked himself.

Before he could decide, the strange lady moved again. She threw one end of the rope over a hook on the wall, pulled the noose down and, still looking at Mrs Lee, put it over her own head.

Mrs Lee just sighed sadly and continued to stare at the empty air above the oil lamp.

The strange lady took her head out of the noose. She pulled the rope down from the hook and moved a step closer to Mrs Lee. Her eyes shone with an evil light. Then she held out the rope towards Mrs Lee and tied another noose. Without a sound, she threw the rope over the hook again, made the noose rope tight and put her own head into it. While she did this, she did not stop looking at Mrs Lee for a moment.

What is the strange lady doing?

'What is that woman doing?' thought Kuo in surprise. 'I shall not leave here until I find out why she is behaving so strangely.'

As he watched, Kuo saw the lady do the same thing again and again. Her face always looked the same, and she made no sound. Mrs Lee sighed so sadly that Kuo felt sad as well. At last she began to cry quietly. Then she stood up slowly and stepped towards the lady. She looked like someone in a dream. She held out her hand. The strange lady's face did not move as she gave the rope to Mrs Lee. Mrs Lee took the rope and threw it over the hook. Then, with one more sad sigh, she placed her head in the noose.

The strange lady did nothing. She just stared at her.

Mrs Lee was just going to pull the rope tight when she knocked against the table. The teapot fell onto the floor and broke with a loud crash. The noise seemed to wake Mrs Lee from a dream. She shook her head and looked around.

The strange lady was very angry. She took the rope and stepped quickly back into a dark corner of the room.

Murder!

Mrs Lee made the oil lamp burn more brightly and picked up the pieces of the broken teapot. Then she sat down again and stared into the distance. After a few moments, the silent lady left the corner, pulled out the rope from her sleeve and again showed it to Mrs Lee. Then she threw it over the hook and put her head into the noose. She did this strange thing again and again. All the time she was staring at Mrs Lee.

At last, Mrs Lee stood up again. She moved like someone who was asleep. She held out her hands and took the rope from the lady. She threw it over the hook and obediently put her head in the noose. The lady's eyes shone brightly with an evil happiness.

This was murder! Kuo could not stay silent any longer. He shouted, 'Hey! Stop!'

He banged loudly on the window. Mrs Lee seemed to wake up from a dream a second time, and she looked around in surprise.

Kuo disturbs the neighbours

All the noise disturbed Mrs Lee's neighbours. They ran out of their houses, asking what was happening.

When they saw it was only Kuo banging on the window, they became very angry.

'That stupid man, Kuo, has drunk too much beer,' they said. 'When he gets drunk, he can't find his own house, so he makes a noise in other people's courtyards! Hurry up and go home, Kuo.'

But Kuo did not listen to the people around him. He was watching the strange lady. She had stepped back into the corner when she heard all the noise. Now she came out of Mrs Lee's house and was running away.

Kuo ran after the lady and tried to catch her. He did not catch her, but he did pull the rope out of her hands. Then the lady disappeared!

Kuo meets the lady

Kuo was quite surprised by this. He slowly wound the rope around his arm. Then he went back to Mrs Lee's house. He tried to tell the angry people about the strange lady, but no one listened to a word. They shouted that he was a noisy, drunken fool. They said that he should be beaten for waking people up and then telling them stupid stories. Hearing that, Kuo stopped arguing with them and ran away. The people returned to their houses. There was silence once more.

As Kuo ran along, he thought about the lady and the rope. What did it all mean? Perhaps there really were ghosts, after all. It would certainly make a good story to tell the others. He ran around a corner in the street. Suddenly the lady was standing in front of him. Had she come out of the dark shadows by the houses? For the first time, Kuo began to feel a little uneasy. Her white face shone in the light of the moon. She spoke to Kuo in a soft voice. It was almost a whisper.

'Give me back my rope,' she said.

A ghost for ever

Her strange voice frightened Kuo even more, but he replied at once, 'I shall not give you the rope. Why are you doing this? Why do you want that unhappy woman to kill herself?'

'I do not want to kill Mrs Lee,' the lady answered. 'However, I must find someone who wants to kill herself. I killed myself once, long ago, and now I have to live in the land of ghosts. It is a horrible place! I cannot leave it to be born again until I find someone else to be a ghost instead of me. If you don't give me back my rope, I will never be able to find anyone, and I will have to be a ghost for ever. Please, please give me my rope!'

Kuo looked at her face. Her eyes were cold and evil.

'I refuse to help you. It would be like killing someone myself! And I know if I give this rope back to you, you will make sure poor Mrs Lee kills herself. I will not allow that! I'm very sorry, my poor ghost, but you will have to find another way to leave your land. Perhaps if you're nice to the ghost king, he will let you live a new life one day. But Mrs Lee is certainly not going to the land of ghosts because of anything I do to help you.' Having said this, Kuo gave a little bow, and turned to walk home.

Kuo's fight with the ghost

The strange lady realized that she could not get her rope back by arguing with Kuo. Her evil eyes shone with a white light. Suddenly she jumped onto Kuo's back and tried to pull the rope from him. But Kuo had wound the rope around his arm, and he held the end of it tightly in his hand.

The strange lady pulled on the rope with all her strength. Kuo felt the rope burning his arm, but he did not let go. He shouted loudly and ran along the street. She was still on his back, and now she was screaming with anger.

'You will never have this rope, you ugly old ghost! Scream as loud you can!' Kuo shouted as he ran. The neighbours heard him shouting again. They came out of their houses and watched him with great surprise. He seemed to be carrying something on his back. But they couldn't see anything there. And he was making a lot of noise.

'That Kuo! One day he'll be so drunk, he'll do something stupid and wake up dead,' they said. 'Look at him! He can hardly walk. His nose is almost touching the ground.'

Too much beer

The strange lady pulled on the end of the rope. She began to pull it off Kuo's arm. He turned and twisted so wildly that he banged his nose on a large stone. He fell down in pain and blood poured from his nose. The lady gave a cry of joy. She jumped off Kuo's back and bent down to take the rope. But just then some blood splashed on the strange lady's dress. With a terrible scream, she disappeared. A moment later, the rope turned into water. Kuo looked around in surprise. He couldn't see the ghost, and he couldn't see the rope, but he could see the faces of his angry neighbours.

'What are you doing, you stupid drunk? Why are you making such a noise? You must really want a beating,' they said.

Kuo did not say a word. He got up, turned around and ran home. When he got there, he jumped straight into bed and fell asleep immediately.

Next day, he was not sure if the strange night had really happened.

'I must have drunk too much beer,' he thought. 'I don't believe there are ghosts. It must have been a terrible dream.'

But then he noticed a mark on his left arm — just where he had wound the rope. It was a dark red mark, like a burn. It took a long time to disappear and after many years, Kuo could still see it.

But even the mark of the rope did not make Kuo change. He still laughed at his friends' stories, and he still drank too much beer. Nothing frightened Kuo for long.

THE BAKER'S WIFE

Help for the baker

Bala is a small town near Ankara, in Turkey. Many years ago a baker had a shop there. He was a poor, lonely man, and he was not very good at his work. His bread was always burnt, and his cakes always looked bad, and tasted worse. Then one day, when he was busy in his kitchen, he heard a noise. He looked up. A lovely woman was standing there in front of him.

The baker was surprised. If people wanted to buy his bread or his cakes, they went to the shop. No one ever came into his kitchen. He was just going to ask her what she wanted there, when she spoke.

'I can bake bread. I can bake cakes. If you give me a bed to sleep in and food to eat, I will bake for you,' she said.

The baker thought for a moment. 'First, bake me a cake,' he said.

The woman set to work. In no time she put a cake on the table in front of the baker.

The baker took one mouthful.

'I don't believe it!' he cried. 'It's as light as air! It's as soft as a cloud! It's as sweet as honey! This is the best cake I have ever tasted!'

Then she baked him some bread, and it was just as delicious. It was the kind of bread the baker had always dreamed of making. He was very pleased. He asked her to start working for him straight away. Six months later, he married her.

The secret

Soon the baker became famous in Bala. Everyone loved the bread and the delicious cakes he sold. People came from miles away just to buy bread and cakes. Everyone begged the baker to tell them his secret. They wanted to know how the bread and the cakes were made, but he just laughed.

'If you want to know how to do it, you must ask my wife,' he said. 'Ever since she came to Bala, I haven't baked a single thing.'

When people asked his wife to tell them her secret, she laughed even more.

'You must ask my husband,' she said. 'Doesn't a husband know all his wife's secrets?'

And so no one ever found out anything.

The baker becomes uneasy

Every night, the baker sat in his garden. He often smiled to himself and thought about his good fortune.

In the three years since the woman had appeared, he had become rich. Now he had lots of important friends. His luck had been very good.

There was only one thing that did not please him. Sometimes, when the weather was very hot, he woke up in the middle of the night, and he was always alone. His wife was not sleeping there beside him.

As time went on, this made the baker more and more uneasy. At last he decided to ask his wife about it.

'My dear,' he began, 'I have a question to ask you.'

His wife smiled.

'Ask me anything. You know I'll answer if I can.'

'Where do you go in the middle of the night, when you leave me all alone?'

His wife's face grew very pale.

'My dear husband,' she said, 'sometimes when the weather is hot, I can't sleep. I just go for a walk; that is all. Now don't bother me with any more questions. Let me get on with my baking.'

The baker did not ask his wife any more questions. But he did not believe her, either. He thought about what she had said all day, and he began to feel very angry.

'Wives should tell their husbands all their secrets,' he thought. 'My wife's baking has made me a rich and happy man, that is true. But what if she's making a fool of me? I must find out where she goes in the middle of the night.'

He decided that the next time the weather was hot, he would stay awake. He would watch his wife to see where she went.

The baker stays awake

A few weeks later the weather became very hot. All over Bala, people sat in their gardens, waiting for a cool

THE BAKER'S WIFE 33

wind to blow. That night, when the baker and his wife went to bed, the baker pretended to go to sleep. He pulled the sheet over himself and closed his eyes. But all the time he was waiting for his wife to get out of bed, so that he could find out her secret.

It was the middle of the night. All was dark. Everything was quiet and still. Suddenly, the baker felt something move. Opening one eye, he saw his wife get out of bed and walk across the room to the window. It was too hot. She threw open the heavy curtains.

Then she said, 'Skin, get off me!'

The baker did not believe his ears. But he had to believe his eyes. Slowly the woman's skin fell away from her, and down onto the floor at her feet. Then, out of his wife's skin, stepped a witch.

The baker turned cold with fear. His wife was a witch! With horror, he watched her fly out of the window into the night sky. He closed his eyes as tightly as he could, and pulled the sheet up over his head. Now he wished he gone to sleep as usual. He had been stupid to stay awake and watch his wife. He would give anything not to know her secret.

He lay there for hours. Then he heard a noise at the window. He heard his wife's voice saying: 'Skin, get on me!' A moment later, his wife got back into bed beside him, and soon she fell asleep. She looked beautiful again, and not at all like a witch. But the baker did not sleep at all that night.

The clever old grandmother

Early the next morning, the baker left his home. He walked along the road to his grandmother's house. He was a little afraid of her, but she was the cleverest person in the town. She had a lot of old books about witches and magic. She would know what to do.

When his grandmother heard the baker's story, she shook her head.

'Why do men always have to know women's secrets?' she said. 'Didn't your wife bring you good fortune?'

But the baker was too unhappy to think of his good fortune.

'Well, didn't your wife bring you money and important friends?' she asked.

But the baker didn't care about his money or his important friends any more.

'God knows I love my wife,' he said. 'But you must tell me how I can stop her doing this terrible thing! I won't spend one more night in the same bed as a witch!'

A handful of salt

The old woman wasn't pleased with the baker's answers. But because he was her grandson, she decided to help him. She looked in all her books, and at last found out what to do.

'The next time you see your wife take off her skin,' she said, 'wait until she flies out of the window. Then take a handful of salt and put just a little on every part of the empty skin. The salt will make the skin stick to her like glue. She will never be able to take it off after that. The beautiful skin will not come off, and so she will never turn into a witch again.

'But be careful!' she added. 'Don't use more than a handful of salt. Any more than that, and her skin will itch for days and days. I don't want your poor wife to feel ill.'

The baker thanked his grandmother, and hurried home.

The baker punishes his wife

That night the weather was hot and still, just like the night before. Once again the baker closed his eyes and pretended to sleep. Once again, he heard his wife get out of bed in the middle of the night. And once again, he saw her take off her skin, and fly out of the window into the sky.

Quickly, the baker ran downstairs to his kitchen. He took a jar of salt from the table, and went back to the bedroom. He opened the jar. Then he stopped for a moment and thought.

'Hasn't my wife been making a fool of me all this time?' he said to himself. 'Didn't she lie to me about her secret? She ought to be punished!'

And the baker poured all the salt all over his wife's empty skin.

Just then, he heard a noise at the window. As fast as he could, he jumped back into bed and closed his eyes. Then he opened one eye. He saw his witch-wife standing over her skin. He closed both his eyes tightly, and lay very still.

'Skin, get on me!' he heard his wife's voice say.

A terrible sight

And then the baker heard a loud and frightening scream. He sat up in horror, both eyes wide open. What he saw then was the most terrible sight any husband ever saw. His wife was dancing in front of him, tearing at her skin. Screaming and screaming, she tore at her skin with her finger-nails, and with her teeth! She tore and tore with all her strength, until she tore herself into a hundred pieces.

The baker jumped out of bed. There were pieces of his lovely wife all over the bedroom floor. He was standing in a pool of her warm, red blood. She was as dead as she could be. He had killed his wife! The baker ran out of his house. He ran and ran through the hot, black night. He ran and ran all through the hot, bright day. By the evening, he was quite mad.

For three days nobody saw the baker. His shop was quite empty and there was no delicious smell of baking. Then on the fourth day he was found by a farmer. He was many miles away from Bala. The farmer said the baker's clothes were torn to pieces. The baker was scratching and scratching at his skin.

'His fingers and hands were all covered in blood, but he just kept scratching and scratching. Nothing could make him stop.'

The baker lived in Bala for some years after this, but he never baked bread or cakes again. The people there often saw him, sitting in his garden. He was as silent and as still as a stone. His hands were always covered with cloth, and tied together tightly with strong rope. That was the only way they could stop him scratching himself into pieces.

The people of Bala were always careful not to look at the mad baker too closely. They knew that he had seen the worst sight any man could see. They were afraid that if they looked into his terrible eyes, they would go mad, too.

5

AFTER MIDNIGHT

A man with big dreams

Once in Bukhara there lived a young man. He did not have very much money. He only had one small shop in the poor part of the city.

But this poor young shopkeeper had big dreams. He hoped that one day he would become very rich and very important. For his dreams to come true he needed to make friends with rich and powerful people.

He knew that there was one thing that the sons of princes and rich landowners always loved to do. They liked to give feasts. Each week in Bukhara one of them gave a big feast for all the others. There was plenty of delicious food to eat, and expensive wine to drink. Each week it was someone else's turn to give the feast.

The shopkeeper began to go to these feasts. Then, one day, it was his turn.

He thought that if he gave a splendid feast, everyone would like him and he would make all the powerful friends he needed. But for this plan to work, his feast must be very good. The food and wine must be even more delicious than usual, and the serving girls must be even more beautiful. How could it be done? Day and night the shopkeeper thought and thought, but he could not find the answer to this question.

An agreement with a stranger

One evening, the young man was in his shop, thinking about his feast. He didn't have enough money to pay for much food and drink. He couldn't ask rich people to come to his small house. Even his serving girls were old and ugly. He began to think that his dreams would never come true.

Suddenly someone tapped him on the arm. The young man turned round and saw a tall, thin man staring at him with cold, green eyes.

'I hear you need someone to help you give a feast,' the man said, softly. 'I can help you. I know all about giving feasts. It need not cost you very much. Will you make an agreement with me?'

The young man felt frightened.
'What do you mean?' he asked.

'I will give a splendid feast for you. It will be the very best feast Bukhara has ever seen. And if you return to your house before midnight, you will not have to pay me anything. Of course, if you stay until after midnight, then you will have to pay a very high price. Do you agree?'

The young man thought quickly. A splendid feast was just what he wanted. And he did not need to think about the money. He would just leave before midnight and so have nothing to pay!

'How do I know you are telling the truth?' he asked.

'Take this ring as a sign of our agreement,' said the stranger, and he handed the shopkeeper a gold ring. The shopkeeper took the ring and saw that it was very valuable.

'If this man tricks me, I will still have the ring. I can sell it and buy food and wine for another feast,' he thought. When he looked up to tell the man he agreed, the stranger had gone.

The feast

On the day of the feast, the young man received a note. It said that the feast would be held in an empty palace behind a graveyard. When the rich young people came to his house, he led them out of the city towards the palace. He led them through beautiful gardens, and over paths covered with lovely flowers.

They hurried eagerly towards the palace, where they could see many beautiful serving girls waiting with dishes of delicious food. They all ate and drank as never before. It was the most splendid feast they had ever been to. They called the shopkeeper 'the King of Feasts'.

As night fell, the shopkeeper grew more and more uneasy. He tried again and again to leave quietly and return to the city, but his rich friends would not let him go. They liked him too much. Midnight came and went. At last his friends became tired, and one by one they lay down in the grass to sleep. Now the shopkeeper was able to leave.

After midnight

He ran back through the night, but it was so dark that he soon got lost. He could not see the road to the city at all. He decided to lie down beside the path and sleep until daylight.

Then he noticed a light shining through the darkness. He walked towards it. It came from a small hut. He knocked on the door. An old woman opened it. When she saw the young man, she gave a cry and pulled him quickly inside.

'What are you doing out there?' she cried. 'This place is full of demons!'

The young man told her all about the feast, and she trembled with fear.

'The man with green eyes is the King of the Demons. The price of that feast will be your life. The next time the Demon King gives a feast like that, the people at the feast will be eating you!'

Hearing this, the young man began to tremble, too. 'Please tell me, what can I do to save myself?'

'Stay here tonight. When daylight comes, run to the city as fast as you can. Then you will be safe,' said the old woman. She gave him a bed, and he soon fell asleep.

Demons and dragons

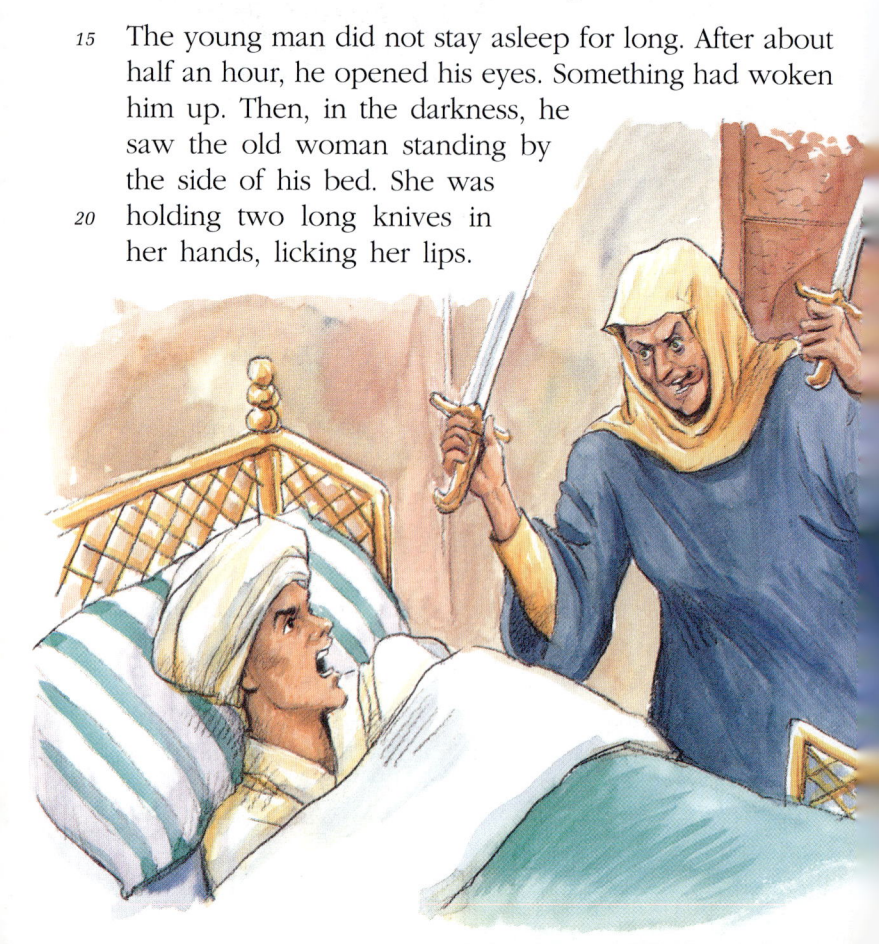

The young man did not stay asleep for long. After about half an hour, he opened his eyes. Something had woken him up. Then, in the darkness, he saw the old woman standing by the side of his bed. She was holding two long knives in her hands, licking her lips.

The young man screamed with fear. He jumped out of bed, and ran out of the hut as fast as he could. The old woman ran after him. She seemed to be as fast as a strong, young girl. She waved her long knives in the air. She shouted at him with terrible anger. She was getting closer and closer. Just then, the young man saw a horse. He jumped on the horse's back and kicked it hard with his heels.

The horse ran off as fast as the wind. Soon they had left the old woman far behind. The horse ran and ran until it reached the desert. Then it ran so fast that it flew into the air. Suddenly fire burst from its mouth. The horse had changed into a terrible dragon.

'It will eat me alive!' thought the young man, and without waiting for a moment, he jumped from the dragon's back.

Help from a priest

The young man fell so far to the ground that when he reached it, he could not move or speak. He lay in the cold desert, looking up at the stars and waiting for another demon to find him and kill him. Then he heard someone coming. He looked round slowly, trembling from head to foot. He looked into the face of a kind old priest.

The priest gave him something to drink, and soon the young man was able to speak once more. When the priest heard his story, he said, 'How lucky that I found you in time. I will take you to see my friend the prince, who lives near here. You can stay with the prince until morning. Then he will help you to go back to the city.'

The young man was so happy that he began to cry.

The prince and his daughters

The prince was an old man with four daughters. He agreed to let the young man stay the night in a tent in his garden. He did not want a strange man to stay in the same house as his daughters.

'In the morning, my servants will take you back to the city. Now, sleep! You are safe here,' the old man smiled.

The young man had just closed his eyes, when he felt a warm hand touch his face. He sat up quickly. This time, when he saw who was standing by the side of his bed, he didn't feel afraid. A beautiful girl was there, smiling sweetly at him with soft, red lips.

'Do not be afraid,' she said. 'Father is asleep, and my sisters and I want to meet you so much. Will you come into the garden and tell us stories about life in the city?'

When the girl led the young man out of the tent, he could not believe his eyes. Three girls were sitting on the grass in the garden. Each one was more beautiful than the next. The loveliest of all was the girl who had woken him, and who now held his hand in hers.

A horrible surprise

Suddenly he didn't feel tired at all. He told the girls story after story, and they seemed to listen eagerly. He was very clever and amusing. He had almost forgotten the demons.

As the sky grew light, they decided to play a game. Each girl would hide, and the young man had to find them. He covered his face with his hands, but through his fingers he watched the girl who had woken him.

He followed her, and when he touched her arm, she turned and smiled. Quickly, he bent towards her and kissed her soft, red lips. The girl smiled even more, and said softly, 'It is after midnight. Now it is time to pay the price.'

At that moment the beautiful girl changed into a terrible demon. It was horrible! It bit his lips with long, sharp teeth, and squeezed his neck so tightly that his face turned blue. The tent, the garden, the house disappeared. He was alone in the desert, fighting the King of the Demons.

The agreement

The young man screamed with pain and fear. With all his strength, he pushed the Demon King away and began to run.

'Where can you run to, you greedy fool?' laughed the Demon King. 'Think of our agreement!'

Suddenly, the young man remembered the gold ring. As the Demon King came closer and closer, he turned and threw the ring in its face. At that moment, the sun rose up into the sky and the Demon King disappeared. All that was left was a snake which quickly hurried away along the sand.

A changed man

The young man ran towards the city, which he could see in the distance. The sun shone brightly, high in the sky, but still he ran and ran. He did not stop until he reached the empty palace, where his friends were still asleep. When he woke them up, they wouldn't listen to his story. All they talked about was how good his feast had been, and who would give the next feast.

The young man never went to another feast. He never saw his rich and powerful friends again, and they quickly forgot all about him. In fact, he hardly ever left his shop after that. He decided that life as a poor shopkeeper was much pleasanter than giving feasts with the help of the Demon King.

6

THE MYSTERIOUS ILLNESS

An unlucky village

Many years ago, in a lonely village in the mountains of old Hungary, the people began to fall ill and die. Every week a line of men, women and children, dressed in black, came out of the little church on the hill and walked slowly to the graveyard. But as time went by, fewer and fewer people walked behind the coffins.

Soon the people became frightened of catching the mysterious illness. They closed their windows and locked their doors. They stayed at home all the time. After a time there were only two people in the village who would follow the coffins — the old priest and the man who dug the graves.

No one knew what the strange illness was, and nothing they did would stop it. The people who caught it had no fever or pain, but for a few days they had terrible dreams. The memory of these dreams seemed to make them weak and helpless, and then soon after that, they died. Everyone in that part of the country was afraid of going to the unlucky village. Fear lay around it like a dark cloud.

There was one other strange thing that happened. In the evenings large bats began to fly silently above the roofs of the houses. More and more of them appeared each night.

The old librarian

News of the strange illness and the helpless village reached the capital city. The old librarian, Balazs, heard about it. One day he packed a bag and rode straight to the unlucky village. He went to the priest's house. He knew that the old priest was still alive.

'You look surprised to see me,' Balazs said to the priest. 'I know I am just an old man. You will think I cannot do much to help. But I work in a library, and I have read a lot of books in my life. When I heard people talking about this mysterious illness, I remembered something I read many years ago. Perhaps I can show you how to stop the people becoming ill.'

The priest listened to Balazs with joy. He was thankful that someone was not afraid to come into the village. No one had been there for many months.

'How did the illness really begin?' Balazs asked. 'Who was the first person to die?'

The priest thought for a moment. 'It is rather difficult to decide who died first. Was it Juliska or her young man, Lajos? Listen. I shall tell you the story properly, one event after the other, from the beginning.'

Juliska and Lajos

The priest began his story. 'Juliska was a beautiful young girl. She loved laughter, and work was like play to her. I often used to joke with her about her future husband. He would be a lucky man to have such a good wife, I told her. I also told her to marry one of the young men of the village. I would be sad if she went somewhere far away. Juliska used to laugh and say that she was not eager to get married. She was happy at home. But in the summer of last year, she agreed to marry Lajos. He was the son of one of her neighbours, and a very good-looking young man. There was no wedding, however, because Lajos had to join the army for a while. Juliska promised him that she would not marry anyone else. She promised to wait for him.

'Last spring, people began to say that Lajos had left the army. They said he was lonely without Juliska, and so he had packed a bag and gone home. But something happened to him on the way back. He must have died near the village, because people say they saw him. We never found his body — just a small bag with his things in it. It was lying somewhere in the fields.

'A few days after the discovery of this small bag, Juliska came to see me here. She came to ask me what to do. She seemed to be very frightened. I tried to calm and comfort her because I knew she was feeling sad about Lajos. I told her that we were not sure that he was dead, but she became more and more unhappy. At last she almost shouted, "I have talked to Lajos!"'

Lajos returns

'Two nights before this, Juliska was getting ready to go to bed, and she was thinking about Lajos. She wished very much that he was with her. It was quiet everywhere and the moon was shining brightly. Everyone else in the house was asleep. Suddenly she heard someone tapping softly at her window. She was afraid for a moment, but when there was another tap, she slowly pulled back the curtain. Lajos was standing outside. His face looked very pale in the moonlight! She opened the window quickly and let him come in. She asked him lots of questions, but Lajos did not answer her. He only smiled mysteriously. Before morning, he left, and that day she heard people saying that Lajos was probably dead. She was too ashamed to tell anyone that he had been with her all night. How could he be dead?

'Juliska waited impatiently for the next evening. Perhaps Lajos would come again and explain everything to her. Lajos did come; again he tapped softly on the window. He looked very pale. Once more he would not answer her questions; but this time his smile frightened Juliska. She asked him to go, but he would not go until it was nearly daylight. After that he came back every night.

'Juliska became so afraid of him that she locked her door and windows. She did not answer his knock. But even when she closed the window, Lajos came into her room. She began to feel ill and weak. She could not tell anyone about her fears. It was impossible for her to tell her parents.'

The first deaths

'When I had heard her story,' said the old priest, 'I felt sorry for her. She was so pale and weak. She did not look like the happy girl I knew before. I talked to her and told her that there was nothing to be afraid of. I said that it was the death of Lajos that was making her so unhappy. It was giving her bad dreams. I tried to comfort her, and at last she felt a little better and went back home.

'The next morning she was dead. It was certainly a sad funeral. A young girl was dead, and perhaps her dear friend, Lajos, was dead too.

'That was how the mysterious illness started,' said the priest to Balazs. 'After Juliska's death, her mother told us that she was having terrible dreams. For a few days she lived, but her eyes were red from her sleepless nights. Then she died, and soon after that her husband died too. And then Juliska's young sister died. Then Lajos's parents and brothers and sisters died, too. After that there were so many funerals I cannot tell you the names of all the dead people.

'Now there are only a few of us left alive in the village. I do not know who will arrange my funeral. I pray that God will let me be the last person to die.'

Vampires!

As the priest told his story, the old librarian listened carefully. Sometimes he smiled strangely and said, 'Yes, yes, that is right.' But the priest did not notice. He was remembering the sad deaths of Juliska and the others.

At last, when the priest had finished, Balazs said, 'I know what has happened here. I have read about it several times. It is not some illness which is killing the villagers. It is vampires.'

'Vampires?' repeated the priest with great surprise. 'You don't believe in vampires, do you?'

'It is not important what I believe. Just think about what has happened,' said Balazs. He was impatient. He wished it was daylight, so that he could start immediately.

'First,' he advised the priest, 'tell everyone to hang garlic everywhere. They must hang it at the doors and windows of their houses. They must also wear some garlic at all times.'

The priest thought this was silly, but he did not know what else to do. The villagers thought it was silly, too. But they did what the librarian said.

'We must open the graves'

'We have a difficult job to do,' said Balazs to the priest. 'We have to open the graves of everyone who died this year. That is the only way to stop the vampires. Write to the government and ask if we may open the graves.'

For several days the priest wrote letters to the government. He described everything that had happened. At last the government agreed to let them open the new graves. Balazs told everyone to cut long sticks from the trees. They had to sharpen the ends of the sticks and make sure they had one sharp stick for each dead body. Then they all went to the graveyard.

There was great surprise when they opened Juliska's coffin. She had died in the spring, a year ago, and yet she looked alive. The same thing was true of all the other dead bodies.

Balazs explained what to do. They had to knock the pointed ends of the sticks into the dead bodies.

The Mysterious Illness

The villagers did not want to do this terrible thing, but Balazs told them, 'This is the only way to free the spirits of the dead people, and the only way you can save yourselves.'

At last the villagers agreed that what Balazs had said was right. The villagers tried to be brave, and they obeyed him.

As soon as they knocked a pointed stick into a dead body, they heard a sigh. Then they saw fresh blood flow from the mouth and nose of the dead person. The body looked really dead now, and a smile of joy appeared on the face.

After they had done the same thing to all the dead bodies, the priest arranged new funerals for them.

They find Lajos

Then began a long and careful hunt for Lajos. A vampire had killed him as he travelled home. When a vampire kills someone, the dead person becomes a vampire, too. Then he goes back to his family and friends (perhaps he is lonely, or he remembers his home) and he turns them into vampires too, even though he does not want to. He goes on doing this until he, himself, dies a proper death. Then his spirit is set free and everyone can live in peace.

For this reason, the villagers hunted for Lajos among the fields and the lonely paths. They found him lying among some bushes. He seemed to be sleeping.

The villagers could not believe that he was dead. They were afraid to knock the sharp stick into his body. However, they knew they must be brave, so they knocked the stick into Lajos's body with all their strength. Immediately, blood flowed from his mouth and nose, and a smile of joy appeared on his dead face.

The villagers gave Lajos a proper funeral, and the village was peaceful again. Balazs packed his bag and went back to the city, and his books. After that, if anyone said that his library had too many old books in it, he would say:

'Oh no! These old books can still help living people.'

7

THE LEOPARD MAN

A hunter with bad luck

When Ngugi was a boy, he dreamed of being a great hunter so that he could marry a beautiful girl. He couldn't wait to grow tall and strong enough to go hunting with the others.

At last he was big enough, and the other men took him hunting in the long grass. But every time he went, he had bad luck. All the other men came home with many animals, but Ngugi always came home without anything. The others laughed and pointed at him.

'If Ngugi tried to catch a tree, he'd have bad luck!' they said.

Ngugi was angry and ashamed. He couldn't understand why he was not a great hunter. Now his dreams would never come true. No one would give his daughter to such a bad hunter, no matter how old and ugly she was. He would live the rest of his life alone.

A visit to the witch-doctor

One day, Ngugi went out hunting alone, and again caught nothing. Angry at himself, he sat down to rest in the shade of a tree. All around him he heard the spirits whispering.

'I think the spirits are giving me bad luck!' he said to himself. He decided not to go home straight away. Instead, he went to see the witch-doctor.

Ngugi told the witch-doctor his problem. The witch-doctor sat in silence for a long time. At last he spoke.

'To be a great hunter, you must be patient. Learn from the other hunters. Practise running after animals and throwing your spear. Practice every day for many years. Then you will be a great hunter.'

This was not what Ngugi wanted to hear. He thought about all the beautiful girls in the village. If he took so long to become a great hunter, there would be none left for him when he was able to marry.

'I can't wait for many years,' he said, impatiently. 'And anyway, I already know all I need to know. The reason why I never catch anything is because the spirits give me bad luck.'

'Not afraid of anything'

The witch-doctor looked hard at Ngugi.

'I know what you want, but it is very dangerous. The spirits can help you, but first you must answer one question. Think hard before you answer. The spirits are listening to you.'

The witch-doctor pointed his stick at Ngugi.

'The spirits ask: what are you afraid of?'

Ngugi stood up tall and straight. Proudly, he said, 'I am not afraid of anything.'

'Many young men come to me, and ask me to help them,' the witch-doctor said, staring into Ngugi's eyes. 'But when the spirits ask them this question, they think very carefully before answering. They are cleverer than you! They know that even the bravest man is afraid of one thing. He is afraid of himself. I can give you some medicine, and then the spirits will help you. But if you drink it, you will be happy only if you are not afraid of yourself. Think, Ngugi! You cannot fight against yourself!'

Ngugi thought — about a beautiful wife. After a few seconds, he said even more impatiently, 'I am not afraid of anything, I tell you.'

No longer a man

The witch-doctor gave Ngugi something to drink. It made him fall asleep for a long, long time. When he woke up, the witch-doctor said, 'Go back to your village. Do not go hunting with the other men. Only go hunting when you know it is the right time.' Ngugi thanked the witch-doctor and ran home as quickly as he could, so he could sit in his hut and wait for the right time to hunt.

Night came, and the village grew silent. Outside Ngugi's hut, it was very dark. Suddenly, Ngugi began to feel very strange. It was the middle of the night, but all he wanted to do was to go hunting. This was the right time!

He left his hut. Outside, even though it was dark, Ngugi could see clearly. He could hear even the smallest sounds. He began to run towards the long grass, and his feet made no noise at all. Suddenly, he found himself running faster than any man could run. Had he grown wings? He looked down at his feet, and what he saw filled him with surprise. His body had changed its shape. He was no longer a man. He was a leopard — the fastest animal in all Africa.

The greatest hunter in the village

Ngugi was very pleased with the witch-doctor's magic. Everyone in Africa knows that the leopard is the greatest hunter of all — nothing can escape it, not even man! Why bother spending long years learning from the other hunters? Now his leopard magic would tell him just what to do.

Ngugi ran silently through the long grass. After a few moments, he heard the sound of gazelles, and decided to chase them. He ran like the wind. Giving a loud roar, he jumped high into the air and caught the leader. He tore out the throat of the big gazelle with one bite of his sharp teeth. Feeling even more pleased with his leopard magic, he dragged the dead animal back to the village and left it outside his hut.

But one kill was not enough. Again and again that night, and for many nights after that, Ngugi ran like the wind through the long grass. In the morning, many dead animals lay on top of each other outside his hut. After a night's hunting, he slept until the sun was high in the sky. When he woke up, he was a man again.

The other men no longer laughed at Ngugi. They said he was the greatest hunter in all the village. One day, the father of the most beautiful girl in the village came to Ngugi's hut.

'Ngugi, you are the best hunter that has ever lived in our village,' he said. 'I would like you to marry my daughter.'

Ngugi smiled and smiled as he agreed. His heart was bursting with happiness. How clever he had been to go to the witch-doctor! All his dreams had come true.

A visit to the beautiful girl

That evening, Ngugi set off to visit the girl he was going to marry. She was at the riverside with her friends. Ngugi carried a basket full of presents for her. He felt so happy, he wanted to run and jump. Soon, the basket began to feel very heavy. This filled Ngugi with a strange anger. He threw the basket into the long grass, and he began to run, faster and faster, towards the river. As he ran, he thought of the young woman — of her bright eyes, her red lips and her soft throat. Bursting with happiness, he ran faster than ever.

When Ngugi arrived at the river, the young woman was bathing with her friends. He walked up and down by the side of the water, not making a sound. How beautiful all those young girls were! Their white teeth flashed in the moonlight as they laughed and played in the water. The one he would marry was the loveliest of all. Ngugi felt very strange. He thought that he must be in love. He was about to shout out to her when suddenly she looked up. She looked straight at him. And she screamed.

A terrible chase

Ngugi tried to tell her that he was not a stranger; he was going to be her husband. But when he opened his mouth, he found that the only sound he could make was a roar. All the young girls screamed with fear. They did not see Ngugi. All they could see was a leopard.

Ngugi's young woman ran away as fast as she could, and Ngugi ran after her. How silly for his future wife to be so afraid of him! He laughed to himself. In his leopard shape, he ran so fast that his feet did not touch the ground. In a moment, he was so close behind her that he could touch her long hair. How could a young girl escape such a great hunter as the leopard? Just one jump, and he would catch her.

Suddenly, he knew something wasn't right. With horror, he realized that he was chasing her just like he had chased that first gazelle. The leopard in him did not want this beautiful girl as a living wife. It wanted to see her dead at his feet!

'Stop!' he cried. 'I will not hurt her!' But his voice was the roar of a leopard. He ran on, faster than ever.

He could not stop himself. Even when the young woman turned her head, and he saw the fear in her beautiful eyes, he could not stop. He fought with all his strength not to jump, but the leopard in him was too strong. Darkness covered his eyes, and he jumped. The last thing he remembered was the taste of blood in his mouth.

Afraid of himself

When Ngugi woke up the next morning, he was a man again. He lay on the ground and cried with anger at what the leopard inside him had made him do. All that day, he lay crying. When the sky grew dark, he began to tremble. At last he understood why the witch-doctor had told him to think very carefully before he said he wasn't afraid of anything. Now Ngugi was terribly afraid. He was afraid of himself, and of the evil thing inside him.

Quickly he hurried to the witch-doctor. The old man was waiting for him.

'There is only one way to end this horror, and the price is high,' he said. 'Offer the spirits the highest price you will pay.'

'I have become an animal! If I continue to live, I know that I will hurt everyone that I love. I would rather die than live as I am now!' he cried. 'I offer the spirits my life!'

Broken dreams

The witch-doctor gave Ngugi something to drink, and he fell into a deep sleep. But he did not die. After a long time, Ngugi opened his eyes again.

'Go back to your village,' said the witch-doctor. 'The spirits are pleased with you. You offered them your life, but they will not take it. You can live like any other man. Be kind and honest. I wish you happiness.'

Ngugi went back to his village. But everything made him remember the beautiful young woman who was now dead, and his broken dreams. He left his hut. He began to go from village to village, doing some work here and some work there, and begging for food and water. Never again in the rest of his long life did he want to go hunting.

8

THE WISE MAN OF NAGASAKI

A wise and gentle man

Mr Sakata had plenty of money. He lived in a big house near Nagasaki, in Japan. He had hundreds of servants. He could buy anything he wanted. But he was not only a very rich man, he was also wise and gentle.

Every day Mr Sakata sat and read in his library. He liked to read about the world and its history. When he was not reading, he loved to walk in the mountains around Nagasaki. As he walked, he would call to the birds and they would fly down to him. Then he would call to the animals and they would run up to him. They were not afraid of Mr Sakata. They would let him touch them, and talk to them. Mr Sakata loved all the animals, even the ugly ones and the fierce ones.

For many years, Mr Sakata lived like this. He enjoyed his life, and he felt very lucky. But after his fortieth birthday, he began to feel unhappy.

'Every day for many, many years, I have read books in my library, yet every day I find there is something else that I don't know. How can I think that I am a wise man if I know so little?' he thought to himself. Then he thought, 'I am getting old. Soon my mind will become tired and my eyes will not see. Then what use will all my money be? There is so much more that I want to learn, but before I can learn it all, I will die!'

The thought of his death made Mr Sakata sad. One day, he was reading an old story about the islands of Japan. In the story it said there was an island far away, where men never grow old and never die.

'I will go and live there,' he said, full of excitement. 'Then I will never die.'

The map

For the next five years, Mr Sakata travelled all over Japan. He went to every city and every village. Everywhere he asked the people if they had heard of the island where men never grow old and never die. But no one ever had.

At last, he came to a very small village a long way from Nagasaki. He went to see the oldest man in the village.

'Old man, can you tell me how I can travel to the island where men never grow old and never die?' Mr Sakata asked.

'Yes, I can tell you,' said the old man. 'My brother went there. Before he left, he gave me a map. I was going to go there too. But I have a wife and family. I love them too much to leave them.'

'Will you give me that map?' asked Mr Sakata.

'I will,' said the old man. 'But before I give it to you, I must tell you two things,' the old man said. 'The only way to go to the island is to fly through the air. No boat can ever take you there. Also, there is only one way to come back. You must walk across the water back to the mainland.'

'Impossible!' cried Mr Sakata. 'But then, I will never want to leave.'

Flying through the air

Mr Sakata took the map. He promised the old man he would look for his brother when he got to the island. Then he set off. He came at last to the sea shore. Far away, in the distance, he could see the island.

'How can I fly there?' he cried. Then he noticed two cranes, circling in the air above a nearby hill.

He decided to ask them to help him. He called to the cranes, and down they flew.

'Great cranes,' he said politely, 'will you carry me over the sea to the island where men never grow old and never die?'

The cranes had heard of the wise and gentle man of Nagasaki, and so they agreed to carry him.

Mr Sakata flew through the air over the sea. After an hour, he was close to the island. It seemed a beautiful place, with high mountains and wide, blue lakes. Mr Sakata was filled with excitement and joy. At last, the end of his journey!

Hell

Soon he landed. After thanking the cranes, Mr Sakata set off to find the old man's brother. But he began to feel uneasy. The people of the island seemed very strange. Some were sitting by bushes, eating berries as fast as they could. They would not stop eating to answer his questions. Some were running round and round in circles. They would not stop running to talk to him.

But most frightening of all were the men with blue faces. They just sat on the sandy beach, twisting their hands together and staring at the wide sea. When Mr Sakata asked them his questions, they turned their blue faces to him and looked at him. They had terrible eyes. He could tell from those eyes that they were quite, quite mad.

At last, Mr Sakata found a man sitting in the courtyard of a house. He did not look mad, and he did not seem to be too busy to talk to him.

'Excuse me,' Mr Sakata called, politely. 'I have just arrived here. I am looking for the brother of an old man I know.'

The man asked Mr Sakata to come into his courtyard, and listened to his story. Then he said, 'I believe I am the person you are looking for. Oh, Mr Sakata, how you will curse the day you met my brother!'

Mr Sakata was very surprised.

'What do you mean? Isn't this the island where no one grows old and no one dies?'

'Yes,' cried the man, 'and I curse the place! You have come to live in hell.'

The biggest fool in the world

The man continued, 'I have lived on this island for sixty years. I came here to study. I wanted to be the cleverest man in the world. But instead I am the biggest fool! Nothing changes here. Not the season, or the flowers; it's impossible to grow a garden. Your own face doesn't even change. You don't yet know how terrible that is. After a while, all you can think of is how to make things change. But it's impossible. Impossible! It is always the same day here. I have lived the same day for sixty years!

'Believe me, life here becomes so boring that you go mad. What a terrible end for us all! The first sign that you are going mad is when you join the men eating berries. They believe that if you eat a million berries, you will grow one grey hair.

Or you might join the men who run round in circles. They believe that if you run in a million circles, you will age by one day. By that time, you will do anything to grow old and die. But there are worse things than eating berries or running in circles. There are fools who try to walk across the water back to the mainland.'

'What happens to these men? Do they die?' asked Mr Sakata, uneasily.

'They fall straight to the bottom of the sea like stones. But a few days later, they are found again on the beach. Their faces are blue, and they are completely mad. At night, they have such terrible dreams! You can hear them screaming from one end of the island to the other. That is the worst thing of all. They live for ever, quite mad, in their own terrible hell!'

Mr Sakata was filled with horror. He had made a horrible mistake. And he could never escape!

A man walks on water

The years passed very, very slowly. Every night Mr Sakata was woken by the terrible screams of the blue-faced men. Every day, he was sadder than the day before. All he wanted to do was to leave this place and return to his house near Nagasaki, so that he could grow old and die.

One day, he was walking along the road when he saw the old man's brother. He was running round and round in circles. He would not stop to talk to Mr Sakata.

Mr Sakata felt so unhappy that he sat down in the road and began to cry. No one even looked at him. After a while he slowly stood up again and stared at the sea. He knew that if he stayed on the island much longer, he, too, would go mad. That was certain. Surely anything would be better than that horrible end! He decided that he would try to escape.

He walked down to the beach, and stood by the sea, thinking. How could a man walk on water? It was impossible. But if he didn't try to escape, he would spend the rest of his life mad, one way or the other! He had nothing to lose.

Just then, he noticed a very big turtle swimming quite near to the island. Mr Sakata had an idea. He called to the turtle, and the turtle swam towards him.

Mr Sakata asked the turtle to help him. The turtle had heard of the wise and gentle man of Nagasaki, and so she agreed. She swam off to fetch her family. Soon a long line of turtles were swimming towards Mr Sakata.

The turtles swam just under the water. When the first turtle reached the beach, Mr Sakata stepped onto her strong, wide back. Then he jumped onto the back of the second turtle. It was just as if he was walking on water.

Cries of joy

A few of the men eating berries and the men running in circles looked up, and saw Mr Sakata. But they were too busy to stop what they were doing. However, when the blue-faced men saw him, they cried aloud with joy. They ran to the beach to walk on the turtles' backs. Laughing and crying, a line of blue-faced men walked over the sea to the mainland, led by Mr Sakata.

When they got to the mainland, the blue-faced men immediately climbed to the top of the nearest cliff. They had dreamed of this moment for so long that they could not wait any longer. With cries of joy that were beautiful to hear, one by one they jumped off the cliff. One by one they died in the sea below.

Mr Sakata watched them jump. Then he turned, and went home to Nagasaki. He found that all his servants had died long ago, and that his house had fallen to pieces. For a few months, he stayed in a hotel in the city. Then one day he left, saying he was going to the sea for a holiday. His body was found at the bottom of a cliff. People say that he jumped.

QUESTIONS AND ACTIVITIES

Chapter 1

Which of these sentences are true and which are false? What is wrong with the false ones?

1 Hoa heard terrible screams coming from the valley below.
2 Then he saw human heads flying through the air.
3 One head flew close to the door and stopped suddenly.
4 It had a pale face, black eyes, long hair, and sharp teeth.
5 The old man said the heads hunted for living people to eat.
6 They used things left outside a house to kill the owner.

Chapter 2

Choose the right words to say what happens in this part of the story.

We (1) **swam/rowed** up the river, and at last we saw a (2) **village/city**. The houses were made of (3) **wood/stone**, and stood on long (4) **trees/posts** in the water. When we arrived, the people came (5) **running/walking** to meet us. They looked at us with (6) **anger/interest** and began talking (7) **loudly/quietly** to each other. None of us could (8) **hear/understand** what they were saying, but they seemed to (9) **welcome/hate** us. We were very (10) **sad/pleased**.

Chapter 3

Put these sentences in the right order to say what happens. The first one is done for you.

1 The strange lady stood in the corner of Mrs Lee's room.
2 Looking at Mrs Lee, she put the noose over her own head.
3 Then she threw one end of it over a hook on the wall.
4 She lifted the rope high into the air in front of her.
5 After some time, she stepped forward without a sound.

Chapter 4

Find the seven mistakes in this paragraph. What should it say?

The baker decided to ask his grandmother where she went in the middle of the afternoon, when she left him all alone. She said that she went for a swim. But the baker did not believe her, and he began to feel very frightened. He thought that wives should tell their husbands all their problems. He decided that the next time the weather was cold, he would stay outside and watch her to see where she went.

Chapter 5

Who said these things to the shopkeeper? Choose from: **the green-eyed man, the old woman, the priest, the prince,** *or* **the beautiful girl.**

1 'Will you come into the garden and tell us stories?'
2 'I will take you to see my friend the prince.'
3 'Take this ring as a sign of our agreement.'
4 'What are you doing ? This place is full of demons!'
5 'It is after midnight. Now it is time to pay the price.'
6 'When daylight comes, run to the city as fast as you can.'
7 'In the morning my servants will take you back to the city.'
8 'I hear you need someone to help you give a feast.'

Chapter 6

Put the letters of these words in the right order to say what the story is about.

No one knew what the strange (1) **lenliss** was. The people who (2) **gatuch** it had (3) **lirbeter** dreams. The (4) **remmoy** of these dreams made them weak and (5) **slesphel**, and then they (6) **edid**. There was one other (7) **gnaster** thing that happened. (8) **gLear** bats began to fly (9) **stellniy** above the roofs of the (10) **oshsue**. More and more of them (11) **parepaed** each night.

Chapter 7

Put the right beginnings with the right endings.

1 That evening Ngugi went to the river to visit the girl
2 When Ngugi arrived, the young woman was
3 He walked up and down by the river,
4 Ngugi felt very strange, and he thought that
5 He was about to shout out to her
6 She screamed and ran away as fast as she could,

(a) and Ngugi ran after her.
(b) he must be in love.
(c) bathing with her friends.
(d) when she looked at him.
(e) he was going to marry.
(f) not making a sound.

Chapter 8

Use these words to fill in the gaps: **beach, circles, tell, blue, bushes, uneasy, running, mad, frightening, seemed, terrible, berries.**

After landing on the island where men never grow old and never die, Mr Sakata began to feel (1) _____. The people of the island (2) _____ very strange. Some were sitting by (3) _____, eating (4) _____ as fast as they could. Some were (5) _____ round and round in (6) _____. But most (7) _____ of all were the men with (8) _____ faces. They sat on the (9) _____, staring at the sea. They had (10) _____ eyes. Mr Sakata could (11) _____ that they were quite (12) _____.

Whole Book

Copy the table and write the answers to these questions in the right places. The name of the most terrifying animals in the world will appear in the centre column.

- Ngugi wanted the (1) _____ to make him a great hunter.
- The man who wanted to marry Juliska, but became a (2) _____, was called (5) _____.

Questions and Activities

- The man with a mark on his left arm, like a burn, was called (3) _____.
- A baker wanted to find out his wife's (4) _____, and put (8) _____ all over her skin.
- A sailor went to China to look for (6) _____.
- The young man who escaped from the valley of the ghosts was called (7) _____.
- A shopkeeper made an (9) _____ with the Demon King.
- Mr Sakata lived in (10) _____ until his fortieth birthday.

Oxford Progressive English Readers

GRADE 1

Alice's Adventures in Wonderland
Lewis Carroll

The Call of the Wild and Other Stories
Jack London

Emma
Jane Austen

Jane Eyre
Charlotte Brontë

Little Women
Louisa M. Alcott

The Lost Umbrella of Kim Chu
Eleanor Estes

Tales From the Arabian Nights
Edited by David Foulds

Treasure Island
Robert Louis Stevenson

The Jungle Book
Rudyard Kipling

Life Without Katy and Other Stories
O. Henry

Lord Jim
Joseph Conrad

A Midsummer Night's Dream and Other Stories from Shakespeare's Plays
Edited by David Foulds

Oliver Twist
Charles Dickens

The Talking Tree and Other Stories
David McRobbie

Through the Looking Glass
Lewis Carroll

The Stone Junk and Other Stories
D.H. Howe

GRADE 2

The Adventures of Sherlock Holmes
Sir Arthur Conan Doyle

A Christmas Carol
Charles Dickens

The Dagger and Wings and Other Father Brown Stories
G.K. Chesterton

The Flying Heads and Other Strange Stories
Edited by David Foulds

The Golden Touch and Other Stories
Edited by David Foulds

Gulliver's Travels — A Voyage to Lilliput
Jonathan Swift

GRADE 3

The Adventures of Tom Sawyer
Mark Twain

Around the World in Eighty Days
Jules Verne

The Canterville Ghost and Other Stories
Oscar Wilde

David Copperfield
Charles Dickens

Fog and Other Stories
Bill Lowe

Further Adventures of Sherlock Holmes
Sir Arthur Conan Doyle